THE DAILY NEWS

THE DAILY NEWS

JEN WEBB

RECENT
WORK
PRESS

The Daily News
Recent Work Press
Canberra, Australia

ISBN: 9780645651324 (paperback)

 A catalogue record for this
book is available from the
National Library of Australia

Cover image: Joshua Oluwagbe via unsplash
Cover design: Recent Work Press
Set by Recent Work Press

recentworkpress.com

PM

To St Jude, patron saint of lost causes, and of hope.

Contents

S1: FIRE

S2: YEAR OF THE PLAGUE

S3: WEATHER

S4: CHANGE

S5: THERAPY

S6: HISTORY

S1: FIRE

First responders

After the apocalypse we sent in the dogs. They moved across the city, sounding the air, finding signs. Below them, cell calling silently to cell, lay the living. All day the dogs kept watch as we hauled the rocks and scraped at soil, fingers bleeding, shovels blunt. We pulled a child from where the school had been; a nun from the church. Three or four we lifted from the heart of stone. We worked all day, pouring water over our heads, coughing up dust, the dogs urging us on until they ran out of things to say. When evening came they fell silent, and walked away, their tails held low.

Driving sober

Another day, another near miss. All the lights turn
red   there's a baby crying in the back seat
a dog and man amble across the road. The car behind me
transforms into cop who is pointing at me to pull over to
the side of the road and take a deep breath and count into
his machine.   Another day another lost chance.   My
hair is lighter now, my eyebrows fading, smoke settling
over my eyes like a ghost gently shouldering me out of the
mirror. I am starting to do what you tell me you do: count
down from 80, figuring how much time I have left.

Apocalypse now

#1

The cyclone lay off the coast, and we taped down windows and mâchéd newspaper into all the cracks in the walls and then hung on, claws in carpet, until the eye arrived, monstrous and still. Above and around us the breathing paused as we called to frightened dogs and dragged loose iron to the safety of the shed. Then it pressed on us again, walls with no door. Birds rose, shrieking, and we lay low, faces in the dust, waiting.

#2

Six pm. The sun shrugs on its dirty red coat but other stars have withdrawn. Your shoes are badly scuffed but who pays attention to such matters these days?

Skin is substance, says the magazine, but I am better schooled these days and know that substance is story, no more.

He says, *That goes straight over your head doesn't it?* If things were otherwise I might feel ashamed, but since we're watching the candle of the world sputter out, there doesn't seem much point in shame now does there?

#3

The wounded world shudders under our hands. It won't be long now: we have done everything wrong and the catastrophe is knocking at the door.

You are transfixed by the slow sinking of island into sea. I am tracing the best path to joy after disaster. If it's true that trauma arrives from the past, then let it come; we're waiting.

Refusing disaster (a survival plan)

The fires blew in ahead of schedule and were gone, and next came the dust and then the storms and then the hail. We unplugged the downpipes we had plugged, scooped dead insects from the pond. Each afternoon you dug out the jew's harp I gave you the year we turned twelve and had it hum and buzz that Nick Cave song about loyalty, the one we danced to, off our tits, the year we turned eighteen. Holding the music in our mouths, breathing out the song. They phone to tell us the funnel-webs are on the move, and we laugh it off, say *everyone is on the move*. The world is growing bigger. I am building a sleeping platform between the shivered trunks of trees while you craft a halcyon garden using only pebbles and ash. They phone to tell us the fires have turned and are heading back our way, and we laugh it off, say *that's not very likely now is it*.

Between the media and the moment

All the inspirational speakers; all the two-for-the-price-of-one offers; every ping on the phone that brings you in from the garden at a run. The blister on your thumb makes it hard to scroll through weary affirmations. Did you or did you not flag your concerns about the current crisis?

He is cyber-stalking you, leaving fingerprints everywhere. You are clearing your caches, deleting cookies, listing false numbers. When you travelled together, and the option arose, he always chose a double bed. When you travelled together, and the option arose, he urged you not to make a fuss.

I won't beat about the bush. The tsunami is upon us and already the roof has left the building.

You can't remember how it was before you were every day filling sandbags. You can't remember how it was when someone else took the other end of the load. Now you have the hospital on speed dial. Now you have the firemen on speed dial. Now you lie on your bed as for a viewing, hands crossed, breathing still.

Fail better

Pour the cognac, a larger tot than usual for this time of day. Your father would frown, if he were here to frown. Cup the glass in your hand, warm against the palm, a subtle move of wrist sends it swirling, and you tilt your head and knock it down in one eyewatering gasp. *Foolish girl,* says your mother's ghost, who is cutting a line, bent over your coffee table and the copy of Beckett you keep there as a warning. Time, that old concertina, squawks out its secret—that even then, it was already too late.

Report from the lab

Despite the fires on the edge of town you *indulged,* as you put it, in *a little light gardening*, and now you are burning inside, the flames flickering through your sultry skin, your smoke-twinged eyes. An hour later and an ice-cold bath and the fire will settle into coals, simmering, shimmering. The rest of your life you will wear the scent of ash, and your hands will scorch lover after lover until you settle for solitude, just you and the cat who curls against your radiance, and the orchid that blooms again, year after year, in the greenhouse of your skin.

Doom scrolling

We wake every day before dawn. First you, then me, and the cats lying in ambush, and dogs with their therapist eyes, waiting at the back door. We wake early and though all I want is sleep and darkened air we head for the banks of the wide still river, *it'll do you good* you always say, needing to see thin sun playing ducks and drakes across the unbroken surface. Caring too much, healing too slow; but that's something we don't discuss. The beat between phrases, birds calling overhead, blood forming tattoos on your wrists. If you would make the first move. If I could open my hands.

The smokejumper starts the day

Earth has made common cause with
fire; the wind is aflame; only water is
still on our side.

Scientists say we
know fire only in
fragments.

Smoke shifts. We gaze into
its heart.

He wakes exhausted from a too-long
night knowing he won't know when
the catastrophe arrives, knowing he
won't be prepared. He eats a bowl
of oats, then drives between banks
of smoke to the station. Ahead, a
car changes lanes without warning.
Ahead, a car pulls off the road.

Scientists say that in a fight the
fire will always win.

Later today he will step into the sky,
and when he pulls the ripcord and his
chute blossoms all he'll hear is the roar
at the heart of the world.

Flames pirouette and jeté.

Blackened grass. Shattered trees.

First responders

I am wearing odd socks, wearing one sneaker, carrying the other in my hand. The sirens have hit middle C and men are ushering us out, shepherds directing their sheep. I have stubbed my foot against something sharp and there's blood between my toes and a shepherd says *don't worry about that now love just go, go.*

I have left my wallet in my room. I have left your photo in my room. The sirens have taken a breath and found F above high C and a shepherd clamps his hands over his ears and shouts *go fuck it this is not a test now go.* I pick up the pace. My wounded feet remember the next steps and shift through first position, third position, a demi-plié and then we're out, the sirens behind us, gasping.

When the news fails

Pack clothes, and toiletries, and medicines. | First aid kit. | Water.
Pack your legal papers, the novel you're writing | your will.

Wool blankets are good. | Also your phone charger, your
jewellery, pens. | Take P2 masks and leather gloves.

Practice packing your car. | It takes longer than you'd think.
Remember to leave space for your pets. Remember pet food.

The roar of the fire as it approaches. | Embers will rain down. It
will be | dark. | There will be no one to tell you what to do.

The last thing you'll hear is | *it's too late to leave.*

Keep the grass mowed. | In an emergency | call triple zero.

Listen to the news.

There may be no news.

There may be no one there to help.

On calculating the value of things

We make the hard decisions: which plants will survive,
which we will abandon to the fire. You have the ledger
in your hand, reckoning the costs, calculating gains.

We're on our way, carrying small treasures to unfamiliar
land. *Do you have a moment?* they ask. *We have a few
questions before you go.*

My grandmother tells me her story. Flight. If not for the
thorns in her feet. If not for the dust in her eyes.

Now she lives with strangers, and a little glass horse she
carried from the ruins. She squeezes limes picked fresh
from the tree and adds a tot of gin, says *there you go love,*
toasting me and my lovely tomorrow.

All night I hear the sirens call. Fires to the north of us,
sickness to the south. It reads like a badly made play.

Sunset

Even in the hardest hours we know moments of peace, fragments of affection that keep the wheels rolling along rough ground as the great world turns, tipping us off balance. I reach for your hand and briefly here we are, facing sunset alongside tourists taking selfies as who would not when the sky is a burst of colour and a contrail makes an untestable claim to be by god the perfect line. I lift my bags and go and you go with me, the smoke settling, cockatoos shrieking their way back home while an insouciant ghost leans against a tree, lighting an imaginary cigar.

The science of kindness

It's one minute before the scheduled departure and she is running up the stairs and up the stairs, across the bridge and down, and as her left foot hits the platform the train is there. Someone helps her on board, someone moves up to make room, the doors close. She'll be home within a few hours, weather permitting, and no clear idea of what is waiting for her there. The train rolls through the suburbs and out into the wilds. The cat in her bag is working its way free and the sun is going down, a silhouette against the flames, and the moon is coming up, red on red. Her phone turns itself off and she places it gently in her pocket, leans back in her seat, closes her eyes. When she wakes again, the cat will be curled beside her, purring.

S2: YEAR OF THE PLAGUE

In March

Gasping. A fish out of water. Wise people haul up the duvet and keep their heads down, knowing what is coming next. Virologists are talking, officials are talking. By tomorrow the whole neighbourhood will have crowded into the local grocer, panic-buying, and you will be hunting your almost out-of-date prescriptions.

What can't be cured, et cetera.

It's like when your loves moved on and you had all weekend to work things out, except that this time the air is Dead Sea thick, sun catching your eye long enough to scald, and Danny next door is making his way up the monkey tree, branch to branch. How will he manage when it's time to go to ground?

White noise

Jelly snakes for supper, water stained with wine. I highstep across sticky carpets to spill all over you. Next door's Gordon laughs like a door slamming, and when the phone first rings, no one moves. The night. Curve of moon odalisques on the neighbour's roof, butters the warm sky. Everyone's phone peeps or beeps at the same moment with the same message—*the cloud is coming your way*, it reads. *Roll up the windows, close the doors.*

Diagnosis

Day one was the fever. First you, then me, and then it was day seven and we moved cautiously, leaning against white walls, hands holding hearts, and eyes. Day ten you restrung your guitar and turned to seventeenth-century arpeggios while I swallowed the last aspirin in the house. By day twelve we had eaten all the snacks. Now you open and close drawers, moodily, and I rattle the windows, hunting the old world. There is a single contrail shimmered against a perfect blue sky, and even through shuttered glass we can hear the chorus of bees.

Nuclear option

There's sun in the carrot you grate across the smoothie you drink each day for your liver's sake. Turmeric leaves your finger stained but you focus on the good it's doing you, your shining eyes that see the world frame by pixelated frame. The sun streams in behind you, making you mystery, haloed on zoom. Take your vitamin D tab each morning like the doctor told you; you can't risk the benison of the sun. You need a holiday; somewhere calm; salt water on your feet.

Liturgy

We collect the box from the garden steps, and spray it down. We unpack fruit and vegetables, cleaning fluids and flour, and set it all in the sun. By afternoon we are washing and storing the groceries, and then we review the day. Routine helps, they say. Empty buses still busy themselves, running routes across the city; bells still call from the last churches standing, and magpies are singing for their supper. And at six precisely, the kid across the road warms up her French horn and plays the Last Post, and all the hours between are left suspended on one unresolved note.

Timetabled

The grocer phones, says they're a bit short; can I wait? The receptionist phones, says the doctor's not well; can I wait? The post didn't come, and didn't come, then all at once it was there and we spent days paying bills.

The scientist tells us her data is lost, the lizards she was tracing are gone, the river she was testing is dry. *This is the price we pay for the future,* she says.

When I balance the books, I'm always five cents short.

The buses have stopped running, and the newspapers, and the schools. The woman walking toward me as I walk toward her steps to the far side of the path, smiles. Children on skateboards, children on bikes, a man walking his dogs: everyone steps aside, and smiles.

It's our keep-fit time, the only hour we spend outside. You opt out, *just for today* you say, and I leave you stretched on the sofa, glass of wine to hand, radio playing quietly. I put on my shoes, open the door, promise I'll be back.

Tech run

We are rehearsing for better days. Each minor syncope hints at a haemorrhage, each cough suggests suffocation. But practice makes perfect, and here we are, balanced on the rim of the bowl. Rivers running past. Milky Way still turning.

The daily news

Morning behaves as though today is any other day, as
though the trees will still respire, and birds sing like flutes,
and artichokes and aubergines cast their flowers and begin
the earnest work of setting fruit. Sun shines blithely on us
all, on the soldier dropped to one knee who is firing into
the crowd, on the young man running across the square,
cradling a wounded child in his arms, on the woman
who cradles a wounded youth in her arms. Turn off the
television. Outside three horses stand watching for you,
ears pricked, then they turn together and run, all joy, and
sun peers between the trees, burnished.

Curfew

Cycle down council paths: people jog slowly, people are walking dogs, walking kids. The air is full of frost but you are wearing coat-gloves-scarf and the bike doesn't care about the weather.

The park is empty, but there are ducks and red-legged waterfowl. Sometimes there's a fisherman, who will yoick a carp out of the lake and leave it on the edge of the path and magpies call all their friends to the feast.

The picnic benches are locked behind chicken wire walls. The playground is locked behind chicken wire walls. The pond is blushing algae, the cascade has fallen still.

Cycle through a silent car park and though you know you are not the only person left alive it takes an effort of will to keep pumping the pedals. When you get to your desk you call your mother and say *it's gone on too long now mum*. It's gone on too long.

At the turn

Here comes the moon, face huge and as blank as the sun. Another month, another moon, and this one with blood dripping from the old man's eye, ears of ancient bunny capturing the kids' attention while moon seeks to corner you, bore you with tales of the all too much it has most certainly seen.

There is no code here to confound but I am lost in origin tales; surely there's meaning somewhere in all this? High overhead, way above the moon, angels are keeping an eye on each other, wondering who'll be next to fall and where the fall will lead. Moon sighs and rolls, lusciously, in its bed of space.

Staying home

He is pacing the little kitchen, and that luscious sensuality
is gone, and though he can still stir the old flesh, it really
doesn't take him to the place he wants to be: where there
is care, where he might feel disappointment or loss or
anything other than gentle contentment, but it's so hard
to rouse the senses when the senses have grown sleepy and
the air thick with rain and the rays of today's last sun; and
there's coffee in the cafetière and he can hear, out of folds
of memory, a cat calling to be let in, and her switching off
the shower, stepping naked and wet and ready to turn to
him, lighting the candle of her smile.

Vexed

The boy with tattoos is leaning over the piano we left outside, playing half the notes perfectly, wincing at keys that are way out of tune. There are, says the doctor, currently 50 deaths per million in childbirth. Which is the best it's ever been. Which is a risk we are prepared to take. Hey Google, says your daughter, what are my odds? *I'm not sure how to answer that*, says Google, coolly.

In the bubble

1.

You stroke the wall until it seems comforted, and I lean
toward you where you stand, the wall against your breast,
just a little in love. I remove my mask, and then you do.
We lean toward one another, trying not to take in the
other's breath, the other's dread, the other's death.

Afterward you call me on zoom and we stare into screens
that resemble each other's eyes. Remembering being in
love. Afterward you call me from the clinic saying you
have had your jab now, when will it be my turn?

The world shakes a little. The trees make sounds that sound
like tears. I leave my phone beside the bed, charging, shut
the door behind me, reach out a hand. And the tree scoops
me against its great self, holds me like a leaf.

2.

What I noticed first was the narcissi in the front garden
turning their faces away when I walked by, and things
went downhill from there. Even the weeds took against
me, resentful unmown grass set trip hazards, bindiis
claimed point position till I cried uncle and began to mend
my ways. They keep an eye on me still, and there are days
I dare not leave the house, but when neighbours ask how
I'm getting on I say *thank you; we are rubbing along all right*;
we are getting by.

3.

All the matter that was folded in my notebooks is swirling in hot easterlies at 40,000 feet, and if I stare long enough and hard, I can see your profile in the cloud. It shifts; you become giraffe, a question mark, a skink.

The blue-tongued lizards have left the garden. Nevertheless I fill their water bowls, the ones you tucked under shrubs before you too left. The clouds have reorganised themselves and are spelling out GO HOME, as though I were ever home, as though I had a home to go to. *With respect*, I say out loud, *with respect*. The clouds blow somewhere else and I will spend the last of the light digging out weeds, while the phone keeps ringing but I can't see where I left it and anyway how will I know if it's you?

Memory crowds the windows after dark, looking for a way in, but I have plugged the gaps with novels and old shoes. I take my light head, my empty head, my synapses that whirr and crank their way through the gears, and move from room to room, checking the locks, testing the doors. If I knew now what I knew then. If I knew what next to do, or who to call.

4.

Cat on my lap, all claws, kneading my thighs, and meantime the phone is ringing and no one is answering and when I mutter into the cat's back you say *oh no no don't go there* so I shan't, I shan't; but still. I have too few followers to make a difference and too many friends for comfort. I have hauled all three bins to the roadside for collection hoping that the strike is over and one at least will be removed. Death rates are escalating and I try to feel the weight of those numbers but can't. Still, when Christmas beetles tap on the windowpane I feel the planet shudder.

There is no carolling this year, no family lunch. I will wrap small gifts and queue 1.5 metres apart at the post office to buy stamps from behind my mask and smile with just my eyes and say *well you just have to breathe it out don't you?*

5.

Here we are, living in *the most vaccinated city in the world* and who can even think of yesterday when today is leaning on us, beery breath down our backs and incontinent *sweetie, oh sweetie, if you knew what I know* in a speech bubble over its head. Call a cab, steer him into the back seat and slap the roof of the car, calling out *I'll phone you, okay?* On a side road, tomorrow is squatting on the pavement, taking a last drag on a fag then flicking the butt into the gutter, straightening up, beginning a John Wayne roll toward someone else's front door. Birds flutter about his head, tweeting. Birds call, heading for their beds, unconscious of the catastrophe that is coming our way. Or knowing they can keep to the air, helpless to help, shaking their heads.

S3: WEATHER

Bureau of Meteorology

Nights when the heat punches down and you, a small frail creature who would blossom under loving hands, throw off the bedclothes, gasping, blood pressed up against your skin looking for any way out. The fan is moving hot air across the room, night fowls are creaking at the gate and the whiskey is gone, and the water, and the kitchen too far to crawl. Close your eyes. The weather will always fail, and the power. You write yourself notes, fear you have been drinking the waters of Lethe. You have forgotten the point you were trying to make.

Wild swimming

How much of you is wild river.

Then there's me, tooled up to meet you

stepping gingerly

through the mud, avoiding

weeds whose aim is to wrap themselves

around me, so close, so strong.

A passion I know

must end in tears.

Monsoon

As the rain fell you remembered other rain; the elephant-foot drops that forced you to steer blindly onto the shoulder of the road and pause, wipers on triple speed, till it eased; or dismal drizzle that went on and on until you banged your head against the door jamb; or rain that meant the drought was ending, fires running out of steam.

As the rain fell you lay face up feeling its fingers on your skin, ants creeping across you to lap the rivulets and carry water back to their tiny dams, bees sheltering under rhododendron petals, waiting for the sun to return, to pack away enough pollen to get them through another month another week another day.

A change in the weather

It was the weather they'd warned you to expect, the wind whispering across the crown of the big tree outside your window, the tree that groans on difficult nights, as do you. On those nights you find slippers and robe and take a glass of Scotch outside, pour out a tot for the tree, and promise Seasol as a chaser and topsoil if it will only give you a hint about how history plays out. Tree has watched settlers become bureaucrats and scholars, has watched El Niño turn to La Niña, and has waited, breathlessly, for fire. Tree has no news to offer. The storm starts up again and behind it the wind, blowing in off the ice, urging you inside to your heater and your bed.

Fort/da

Ice where it ought not to be. Doors that no longer lock. The cats are crying outside the window, the baby is playing in a darkened room, and I am hunched over my phone, tapping out your number, pressing End Call before the first bell rings. Outside the clouds are roiling. Outside corellas are shrieking. I make myself small, creep to the back of the pantry between the onions and the sacks of rice, and hum consoling sounds, waiting for the storm to surrender.

Laws of physics

Bicycles spin down dual-use paths where pelicans lift their heads, their shopping-bag beaks like a song someone has forgotten to sing. I cycle slowly along the edge of the lake, past the busy marsh hens, determined to avoid the shriek of siren, frightened faces on strangers who'll stare down at me saying *are you okay?* We have been here before. We have lifted our broken bones with no more than muscle and shame, crawled to small caves where we could lie, and lick our wounds, and slowly heal. Lover, I am here now, expecting nothing but tomorrow's sun, an autumn breeze, another day.

Seachange

The boat draws up to the jetty, meringue seething at its stern, engines shouting *Back! Back!* and you take the deckhand's hand and jump ashore, shoulder your bag, begin the hike down the headland. The water looks edgy, and beyond the breakwater it's going right off its face: lowering skies, sweaty gales. You struggle into a sou'wester and now the sea is licking the edge of the road. It is watching you. Do you take shelter? Drop your bag and run it's only three miles home? Or continue all straightback dignity as the waves begin to sniff around your feet, the bag digs into your shoulders and look, here comes the storm.

Rewind

We're up against it again, and the green breath of day is going full virus across words we thought we could say. Letters are vanishing, world becoming wor d, love merely lo .

Control-Z can't fix this mess, can't undo decisions we have made and made again, knowing there was no future in them. No future with a paragraph into which I could pour myself, a desk where I could settle down, hit shift + return.

Rolling the dice

In snake season we crash-bang through grass as high as my waist. Make a noise, your grandad would say, and all the wild things will slip away. In winter I spend silent evenings playing cards, handling both hands, gambling against my own game. You stand on the verandah watching the dark for whatever might appear. In spring darkness, there's marigold and poppies, asparagus fronds, and shaggy gums. In autumn there will be wildcat spoor among the tomato plants but if you don't see it we'll be safe. Thistles fight back when we appear with leather gloves and trowel, or that's what you say, here in this garden of trees and weeds, this new world we don't yet love.

Staying home

It is raining, slow dry rain that fills our dams with air, bringing ants and turtles from their nests to bathe luxuriously slow, and dry. Last week the sun, yesterday the storms, tomorrow could be anything. Bring in the wet laundry; greet the nodding trees. Today is the weather to spend in odalisque mode, half-propped on pillows, the cats running errands, my legs stretched against yours, my open book making eyes at you.

Mushrooms

I wake from a dream of raspberries to find the bed turned to slurry, the walls a decadence of red. Someone in the next room is typing too fast, hitting keys, missing keys. The air is salt, a mangrove swamp at low tide with ibis highstepping through the mud. The senator is knocking on the front door but I am measuring the mycelium, field notes growing at the rate of rot.

Weekender

Rain is painting the roof dark grey and you make a virtue of necessity, sitting cross-legged on the spare-room floor and sorting nails and bolts and screws into proportionate piles. I in the kitchen am stretching out sourdough, measuring by hand how it changes from sticky to silk, accommodating wheat and water and air. A magpie taps on the glass, one for sorrow, and you appear at my side, claiming the scales which I know odds are I won't see again, like the kitchen scissors, the aspirin jar, the book I was reading last week. I watch you weigh and count the bits of steel, sort them into little jars, slide the jars into boxes you will store in the old wooden wardrobe in the shed, where odds are they will remain until someone else unpacks our lives.

Being there

Clouds tack ahead of the gale and there's a high thin voice on the wind. We can't tell if it's a siren or just harmonics on the sound waves that clutter the air. Stretch out beneath the neighbour's hedge where rosemary reminds you that nothing really matters but the moment, not even when the neighbour's dog checks out whether you belong here, not even when the promised rain pelts down, drenching you through your garments, through your skin, deep as the earliest memories of breathing through fluid, the thrum of a body you no longer know. It's getting cold but you stay put, slipping into a dark rest, and the neighbour's cat has settled on your hip, claws out and purring, small satisfied sounds that rock you roll you into sleep.

S4: CHANGE

Cherries

The lyrics shift between *You're dreaming* and *You're dead*,
but all he hears is the tone he draws from skins, from slabs
of stone. He has fingers and sticks to drum with, mallets
and brushes and rods. He has cymbals and shakers and
wires.

He is tapping out the rhythm of the dream that woke him,
the heartbeat of the air they both breathe. *You said what?*
she asks, turning over in bed, pushing the sleep mask from
her eyes, and he puts his hands on mute.

Now he stands at the cold window, tapping out the
rhythm of the cold night, watching a solitary possum
tightrope-walk the power line between street and roof,
remembering the cherries he left on the bench outside.

Tree changing

We packed our books and plates and hit the road, heading
for a home where hens and gardens could spread across
unmown lawns. You chose to pack whatever promised
joy, I packed trowels and hoes and sheets. After we settled
in, we said, we'd take turns preparing meals, scouring the
stove. Take turns collecting fresh laid eggs and bringing in
linen scented by the sun. Nights we would drape ourselves
across the bed, skin to skin. I try not to picture the next
move, the next journey to untried ground. Not sure I have
another move in me. Not sure I could let you go alone.

Nature morte

I acted art for you, being now nude duck descending a staircase, then man walking to the sky, then Oldenburg's giant peg. You swore that art would open doors, but it was never likely to be true. Poised as a Morandi I wait indoors, watching the damaged world, breathing the barbeque scent of a continent ablaze. The house is filled with all you left me before you left me. Chocolates uneaten in the fridge. Negatives fixed and washed, still on the drying line. A string bag of oranges, slowly turning brown.

Strange attractors

Once the moon arrived the party got going, oboes against the hedge, dancers on splendid heels spiking the lawn. We should have mown the grass, should have raked the leaves and bark. Weeds boil through from next door's yard, ivy muscling over the fence, and birds strafe the yard with elm blossom, its buttery petals confettied across the ground. The moon shrugs it off, comfortable in its own skin, happy to watch humans wrench meaning from music. Moon eavesdrops on the overwrought stars and their exaggerations; it bets on the origin of each satellite that spirals by. You have hauled a deck chair to the edge of the lawn and are lying back, giving yourself over to the evening, tracing paths across the lines of the sky.

Night watch

Twilight; the birds aren't yet in bed but the bats are out.
Five streets away traffic hums in three-part harmony and
the last helicopter of the day has turned on its heel, heading
for home. You are pacing the edge of the road, semi-blind,
feet fumbling across cracked pavements. You startle at
something that sounds like a shotgun on the other side.
The dogs fall silent, parsing the sound, then one starts up
again, near you, and the whole choir joins in. Pavement
turns to field under your feet. North unexpectedly looks
south. One eye out for dogs, you pick up your pace,
looking for light.

Autumn

Leaves mutter quietly to themselves
          as they fall. We hear them above the traffic's hum
        a sound like bees
    a sound like the deep secrets no mammal can decode. Like
        how to pollinate, or
           what rocks debate in their century-long sentences.

           We are walking home, all we own carried on our backs
        or all we care about owning.
    Cockatoos prune the cherry blossoms,
  the lawn has become romance,
our front door the colour of the sea.

Swimming the reservoir
(for RD)

Every morning any season you go barefoot on feet that once were tender but now have learned to live with pebble and thorn. You pick a path through shrubs and stubble, putting up marsh hens and the occasional roo who steps out of reach and watches you make your way down to the concrete wall and the water that holds the sky in its arms and holds you too, first in reflection and then in truth as you plough across and back, across and back, watched by pelicans who sail alongside, watched by water skippers who need no introduction and by the midges you will try hard not to harm. Back on land you watch your own form sheet off your skin and back into water, then gather reflection and true self, knowing that the gap between them is crossed by the bridges that you tread.

Stellar

Insects circle the scene, and the cat leaps at them, all grace and rampant claws. You are outside, saving bees from the birdbath. You are outside, sweeping a path from kitchen door to the ants' crumbling nests. The cat follows you, calling, and the phone is ringing, and impassive stars rise and set. If you could simply sit and watch the night sky blinking steadily at the earth you would live forever, or at least until the end of this age.

On the fault line

The ground is shaking, and the neighbours are stressing out, and I flick the switch on the kettle and rinse cups and trays. Last year's smoke still stains their walls. *No lives lost though could have been*, says Mike from next door, tapping his index finger against the table. *No fires neither*, says his mum.

The air turns to sludge, soil becomes water, and we are swimming between the flags, hoping the lifesavers have their eye on the tiny flutter of hands above the swell, bright orange swimming caps hauled over untrimmed hair, loud rubber flowers making a point about us being sixty plus but still willing to give it a go.

Futurist

The child sketches water, a longboat moving under the energy of song, fire kindled in its stern. He grows grave and includes a tiny steamer, a paddle that eggwhisks the sea and enlivens the ceremony of farewell. *In years to come, his grandfather told him, they will describe us as the past.* Now grandfather is in his lead-lined bed, pumped up with formaldehyde and looking, his daughter insists, twenty years younger. The child has only a breath to realise that this is what people always say not knowing what to say in the face of sadness and silence and the steampunk future that is waiting for us all.

Solstice

Snakes are sleeping in the leaves that have Monet'd the back lawn. We step carefully along the path, waiting for late spring when they will stretch out of sleep and up to the finally warm air, then head off we hope to breakfast elsewhere.

Mice are nesting in the compost bin, nibbling our discarded bread and greens and corn. I need to shovel up the last of the quinces. Need to cut the shards of summer plants, mow the grass, turn the soil.

Rugged up on the verandah we watch the new season unscroll, icy moon scattering frost on morning cars, ferns turning black as winter takes its hold. In six weeks the sun will return, the day will stretch out of sleep and open its doors to the new warmth. Your arm across my shoulders. This endless time, and against it, bashing tiny fists upon the pane, my little life.

On the agenda

The river has changed its path and flows past the office where I used to work at my sit-stand desk, or lean back in my wheeled chair, wondering what to do next. Koi swim upstream and open their tender mouths, and I scatter fish food and crickets and lucky coins for their pleasure. During the rainy season we shut the office and put a notice on the door, urging customers not to call. In the dry season I fling open windows and doors, breathe in mangrove scent. Most days I get a message from the boss, patient questions about the progress of this budget or that report, or why I didn't show for the meeting I was expected to chair. I am hoping for an offer to retire. I am hoping to slide like they warned me into obscurity, waiting for mornings spent watching basil grow, afternoons wrapping sage into smudge sticks, no more creditor demands, no more warnings from the medical centre that my mammogram is five years overdue.

Harmonices Mundi

We are singing, the whole choir, under moonless sky. Music is shifting shape, banksia man slowly turns his head and clears his pipes, then a one and a two and a three shiver his languid limbs. Bark drifts slowly, trying to syncopate while the magpies carol out their version of the mazurka. Eventually even the planet deigns to join the choir, throwing back its head, letting the sound rip. We can't hear it, but still we know it, the music into which we were born, the universal key.

S5: THERAPY

Materials

I am everything your mother told you and none of that. Every scent from the boronia bush you have been nursing through violent summers and violent winters over these past years. I am the cat who presses her head against your throat, and purrs. The sun who holds his breath during each eclipse. I am all those years when men returned to their rockets to orbit back to earth, bringing moon dust in their beards and in the tread of each boot. The stuff of which you are made.

Saving the planet

Your heart beats lub dub under my grateful hand while
the world is practicing Buteyko and a skink has found the
sticks we propped in the birdbath and hauls itself hand over
hand to solid ground. The girl next door is playing scales
on an alto horn, I can hear her quick intake of air between
C sharp and E. *Practice*, her mother says. *Practice*. Your
heart, a metronome, beats out three/four time at a steady
middle C, and the girl next door misses a note, honks off
key. If you were awake you'd laugh no doubt or cross the
fence to correct her stance. You breathe on, deep sounds,
slow sounds, sounds the world makes as it moves into the
difficult stretch, murmurs *omm*.

Studies on Hysteria

After all the warnings it's the spilt milk that brings us to
our knees; the mislaid wallet, the broken pen, the switch
that keeps fusing. It's the principle, we tell ourselves, of
camels' backs and last straws, but who knows which of the
ten-a-penny crises will strike the final blow?

You are stretched out on the doctor's couch, practicing
slow breathing as he counts you down to ten. Then, *worst
fears?* he asks; and when you think you have responded
he says—*now consider something worse.* You consider. Then
press pause, amazed by how far fear can take a person.
Amazed too how despite it all one can remain entranced
by the patterns of bees' wings as they move, studiously,
from bud to bud.

Alternative medicine
(for John)

You are outside among the trees, hands on aching head. I am tidying the kitchen, checking new loaves as they rise, noticing that I am losing my sense of taste and that the more I cook the less there is worth eating. Now you press your forehead against the tall gum tree; scientists say it can extend one's life by years or at least make life more satisfying, like eating dark chocolate, or drinking single malt, two hundred dollars plus per bottle to prove its worth. You swirl a single tot in a wide mouth glass and breath in its bouquet, being unable just now to gulp it down, the rapid tip of wrist to mouth, the heady burn, heat rolling down through the flesh confirming that life still has its savour, that the pain will pass, that you will press naked feet into the deep litter of bark and leaf all scurried about by wildlife, and remember what flesh says to world, that we are here today, touching you, learning to breathe you in.

After the party

Like coming home three sheets to the wind when you'd
promised to behave, keep your cool, keep your calm, not
make an exhibition, et cetera. You remember yahooing
half-balanced on a roundabout while some guy you met
at work jockeyed it along till you let go and let centrifugal
force do its work. Your stockings are torn, and the skin on
your palms, but frankly you had, you tell him, absolutely
the best time ever. He turns, and you can't quite catch what
he said on leaving the field.

Second sleep

You are asleep under a scatter of silk cut and I would never let you know it offends. Mother always said if you can't say anything nice. When you wake at three-thirty I will be sleeping, and the neighbourhood, and the cats, but you will rise nonetheless, lay out the cards, five of wands over nine of swords. And if the power goes off you will find your lighter and beat back the night with its little flame, the gleam it casts across the shadows as you tread quietly through the house, shutting the fridge door, switching off screens.

Everyday myths

Possums on the roof begging with menaces; currawongs
tapping scimitars on the doors. I am tuning myself to the
more-than-human world, becoming bird, and there's a
stranger advancing on me, net in hand. It's Myth #5 in the
full-length Joseph Campbell I clutched, sputtering, while
my teacher chanted at me. I don't want this pounding of
thought and sensation, anxiety of influence, inattention.
My new lover appears in the room, bringing champagne
and tales of the tiny outdoors, images of where we might
be if we could jettison the flotsam, clear the surfaces, start
again.

Working it out

We took the challenge, and within weeks were at the doctor, running on machines, gasping out *too fast too hard* while the nurses said *run! make it count!* Next we took an easier line: oatmeal for breakfast, coconut oil on our skin. *Do I smell weird,* we asked each other and each said *no, you smell fine.*

I wish we had a more urbane life, you said, but we both know that's not likely now. *Strangers are coming your way,* said the fortune teller, *though they aren't the handsome kind.* She folded our palms closed; she refused our coins. Now we are concentrating on paying off the mortgage, putting out the bins. This is not the life we thought we'd be living, but at least we are living.

The future of illusion

She's struggling to get closer to the sun, sure she could begin to understand, despite the flickering of attention and the texture of the hot air scratching at her lungs. *Understand what?* asks the therapist but she only shakes her head, fumbling to shape words that will fit in her mouth, words she can roll around her tongue, let fall onto the table where he keeps his desk calendar and the photo of his favourite car. She spits them out onto the blotter and plans to arrange them into sentences but stands, instead, and leaves, very gently closing the door.

Refuse/refuge

The verandah tipped to the north and she went over too and lay on the sweet timbers staring into the eye of the world, which she later realised was no more than the shining moon on the edge of the neighbours' roof. And in fact the verandah had not tipped, she later agreed, in therapy, but she had; or had *been tipped*, said the counsellor, though the passive voice distressed her. Not that it matters from this distance, time having done its tricksy thing and cantered away before returning like a curious horse to check out the mess it left behind. She reaches out a hand and clasps the rope someone has draped across the sky, hauls herself to her feet, begins again.

Above the Mariana Trench

Adrift in calm water. Clouds say there's weather coming, but we are out of range, longitude 16°41'28" N, latitude 147°48'12" E, and far from shore.

Always hopeful, you turn the dial. The soundwaves are full of storm and evensong, that litany of islands, of pipe and port. You twist the dial.

I am feeding out the lead-line, seven thousand feet and counting. *The higher you go, the further you fall.* Keep turning.

The microphones report nothing; and the radio reports nothing; and the line passes twelve thousand feet, thirty thousand feet, and the sea is lying doggo and I've run out of line but haven't reached the floor. I stare at my hands. I stare at the coil. I wait for someone to tell me what to do next.

From the family album

The sun has left a watercolour wash across the sky, and birds are flying nestward. We have poured the second wine of the evening and placed an order of pho for two. You are fretting about folk in distant nations being slaughtered by soldiers or lacking water or watching the glaciers fade. The child is fretting because his cracker has shattered on the kitchen floor. I don't know how to help, not when you look at me, something unreadable in your gaze.

Beyond the Pleasure Principle

The doors open and close, so many people on the move. My therapist handily deals out a deck of images and then scoops them away: *What did you see?* I open my eyes and see colour, I close them and see black. Tell me a story? *No.* He spreads the images out again, palms and fingers splayed to shatter the shapes. I see the curve of shoulder, someone's lovely haunch, an open mouth. The doors open, then close; the black behind my eyes is fading; sometimes a door is just a door.

Irrational fears

That when I look in a mirror, it won't be me looking back.

Spiders: that's a common one. The greenies in my street have posted flyers, urging us to toss out poisons and live at peace with our pests.

That when I look in a mirror there will be someone or something just behind me.

Clowns, inevitably. That *they* will find out. That next door's dog knows more about us than we are willing to reveal.

Birds. I guess because of evolution.

That you will leave me, or die; either one. Or that you won't.

That sometimes, when I look in the mirror, there is no one looking back.

S6: HISTORY

At the Clockmakers Museum

They have moved us to a new room, where the changing quality of air plays merry hell with our workings. Still, says the keeper, a bit of oil, a bit of a rub, you'll be back to normal. To what counts as normal. You, creaking yourself upright and bowing at the waist; me, inclining my head and my eyes, extending elegant arm. Your timber meets my steel, and element calls to element. I have loved you since 1823. *In the last analysis*, you start to say, but the wheels stutter and stop, and I will never know what happens next.

The passage of time

If a dog should bark. If thought should drift like paper
fallen from the roof—a brief flutter and then nothing. The
moments of the day coil themselves up, a damaged spring,
and then tilt slowly to one side.

The event crept up on us, no herald's call to announce its
arrival, its leaving. Only its Cheshire smile remained as
evidence of its passing. That, and the shadow of its turn,
and the ragged end points I must knit together.

Hens look up from their grain, then retreat to the roost as
rain falls quietly out of a blue sky. I can't make sense of it,
but you, growing magisterial, announce that the absence
of news is the passage of time—as when a dog fails to bark,
as when the postman does not call.

The cat is asleep in the doorway. I curl up beside her,
muted, and we sleep together undisturbed through events
we had not foretold.

Automaton

Silver swan on glass rods turning clackclack, silver fish leap between the rods till swan snatches them up, mmm breakfast. Outside it's a short journey from sublime to ridiculous and some ape is beating his chest and howling, wild birds fly up in a mime of fear, and between woodpile and fence a bluetongue lizard is going about his business. Back inside. You have been training for months to learn precisely how to key the silver swan, how to wake it from two hundred and something years of somnolence. It's just a machine, says your ex, collecting the children and their overnight bags, but he has never seen it stretch into life, reach out its lovely beak, never seen every feather and tendon settle and shift. You could watch it all day, but the curator is coming soon to remove it and you will have to learn to look again at the living world, as we drift from mammal to machine and back.

Dewey decimal

It was because of the holes in the fabric, and what she could see when peering through torn panels. Because when asked to explain herself all she could do was move her hands, inconclusively, and stutter out sounds.

Now you have marooned her in the Book of Mourning. Sometimes you leave it on the bedside table. Sometimes you riffle through the pages where she waits, endearingly still, and you knock back another shot and think of you and her, and set the book back on its shelf.

As if this were not the last hoorah. As if this were not the last time you will touch her.

Foreign affairs

Because I speak Sumerian as though born to it, because grandfather was a minor prince, because when the Russians come I will sing their anthem pitch perfect, they chose me to learn the arcane semiosis of spy. Now, fully schooled, I move like a cat, knocking treasures from shelves, leaping slo-mo across the abyss. Each new task knocks one more life off my list but the joy of knowing, the hunting and the finding, keep me on the prowl. Poised for the next adventure.

Early morning

Sweep away the frost: the car and the steps and the spinach plants are white and you are shivering. You'd rather stay in bed, drink coffee brought you by kind lover, eschew the world and all its KPIs. But hope is dished out in coffee spoons, your favourite city has just collapsed under the weight of inertia, and you are without a slide rule to hand.

We know that something has begun. We know we are in it for the duration. Now the sun is higher; now the early morning race to the office is done. Pick up your lunch pail; find your keys. The days of your long durée have arrived.

At the Lifeline Bookfair

He places his hand across a stack of books no one has noticed. The next table bears a scatter of foxed military history and across the hall is sci-fi, stacked twelve deep. It's not my genre, I am explaining to the stranger following me, and he interrupts to say—*but who'd have thought that the future would come at us so fast?* Twenty years is a lifetime says an elderly man and I calculate how many he has enjoyed, counting on my fingers, pretending I am not wondering whether I have even one left. Last year's calendars are up against the wall, $1 a pop. To scroll back as well as forward. To see the future coming at you like a rhino, and still hold your nerve. *Can I buy you a coffee* asks the stranger and I say yes, yes you can.

Sounding the hour

We mute the light, saving our eyes for more demanding sights. We don wrap-around specs, switching off lights, drawing the blinds. The garden is gasping for rain, the currawongs calling out for summer, and I don't know if I'm ploughing my own furrow or digging someone else's grave. But though the news is not good this week, your favourite cat still comes calling, winding between your feet, humming her content. The anchor looks as solemn as someone playing his own fugue and yes, the Doomsday Clock is set at almost midnight, but our grandchildren, those entitled innocents, will have reached watchful middle age before Big Ben starts to toll the end, and by then I will be gone, and you.

Riding the Greyhound

Passengers stumble between seats, clutching strangers' shoulders when the bus jolts. They open the door and stumble down the steps to the metal washbasin and the metal toilet stool and the metal mirror that mirrors you as you might be if you live a lot longer and get no rest. There's a notice on the wall, a damp roll of paper, a light switch. Nothing else but a vent that breathes patchouli. The bus rolls on like the toddler's song, approaching the border. You have no passport and no nation that will give you one. You twine your fingers, rehearsing the narrative you've prepared.

In Berlin

I kissed you at Checkpoint Charlie below placards of guards knee-deep in ice while youths handed us leaflets for two-for-one meals. I kissed you outside the Hauptbahnhof and you checked your watch and said there was just enough time to catch the last entry at the Reichstag. At Alexanderplatz a tap dancer approached me, *percussively* you said, and I watched her through the lens, one hand changing focus, the other reaching for beer. A stake in my chest, crowds outside the windows at Kadewe, where *look!* you said, pointing, but my field of vision was shrinking, the pavement looked so good, I curled there, thumb in mouth, favourite scarf against my cheek, watching the river rise.

History for beginners

It's the way my own history clangs up against the rest of the world

<kapow!>

<biff!>

<ka-zooie!>

which would be almost funny except
(stories beyond what is tellable

shame rising

you twirling a hank of my hair around one thick finger…)

So I sit in the bathroom, wedding photos burning and curling in the basin
    sit in the bathroom watching my smile and how
      the flames flicker across my stupid eyes
floor tiles lethally slick, mirror foxed around the edges
steam forgetting itself it sinuates across the ceiling—

there is an emu in the sky   there is a man
          with dogs, with lethal bow
    there's a bear
    cluster of sisters
        parliament of stars ….

*   *   *

You draw the blinds, say *that's enough for now.* You
reach out a hand, promise distraction, but a spider
is making its exhausted way across the rug, flanked
by cats who wonder whether to make their move.

They make their move
you turn off the light, you say *that'll do for now, love.*
That'll do.

When memory fails

You see me and if prompted you offer up my name, a gift. I bring you cakes on a little tray, sweetening the blow. We rehearse the chat we had last night, and this morning, and will have again later today. Time is ground down to the bone, but still it expands, a stretched balloon, then unscrolls, a hamster in a wheel.

Each day is the first day. You have become river, each moment made new. I slash rank grass from the riverbanks, set out stepping stones for you to follow. At night I keep watch. Daytime I make the call, betraying you, marking time.

Eulogy for a dead lover
(for TS)

The alarm clock rings, and you roll over in the bed and then remember what this particular date means, and you know there's no day in the calendar that doesn't signify for someone, but this one digs its fingernails into you, and twists. You remember the wild and perfect times; their traces drift through the atmosphere mostly forgotten; which disappoints you—all that, and no lasting effect— though you know that you too forget it, remember your long-ago lover only occasionally, missing him at those moments when he's the only one who would know how ridiculous is the thing that just happened, would know how hard you try. Old photos tell you it was neither miracle nor mistake. Two streets away the bells at the Buddhist temple start to sound, their tone shimmering through houses and gardens and sheds to settle somewhere below your solar plexus, and you feel your pulse shift to meet the pattern of the chime. You let go; you think *I can't let go*, but then you do.

A history of speech

I like a door that sounds decisive when you close it a child who knows precisely when to hang up the phone the historian who discourses on the use of 'hang up' for the phones we now use my rusting memories of lying on the floor of my parents' bedroom spiral-wired phone against my head listening to you breathe while you listened to me breathe as though we were rehearsing for a future we would not live to see.

Leaving love behind, you place the phone back in its cradle. Leaving love behind, you close the door. So gently it might have been a breath.

Afterword

Scientists and philosophers have been discussing the Anthropocene for decades now. In 1824 the physicist Jean-Baptiste Joseph Fourier published a paper that observed that our planet should be cooler than it is, based on our distance from the sun, and across the 19th and 20th centuries, measurements and observations and theorising made it clear that something was wrong with the Earth. In fact, human beings have been considering the climate as well as the weather since the ancient world; and the Enlightenment cranked up the pace. Montesquieu famously wrote and spoke about the centrality of climate, as did Abbé du Bos and Comte de Buffon and others—though not in an ethical framework we would now applaud. They wrote extensively about the impact of different climates on the people who live under its rule, failing to note the impact of human activity on the climate—but it is still a useful stepping stone along the path to recognising that humans are part of, rather than distinct from, the material/natural world.

The late 20th and now the 21st century have been characterised by fierce squabbles about the nature of climate change—or, indeed, its very existence—and a shift in discourse about the role of human beings in the global ecology. This is evident across the sciences, and in the social sciences as well as humanities and arts disciplines. Political scientists John Dryzek and Jonathan Pickering, for example, urge us to listen 'not just to human voices, but also to the non-human components that cannot speak like humans do—but to whose signals we can try to listen better'. And after listening, they say, we should reflect, recognise and respond to the cries of the world—that is, engage in a process of reflexivity that (you never know!) might mobilise political and economic change.

The poems in this collection arise to some extent out of my considerations of the scholarship on the topic, but not consciously: they are the product of me living through recent years of floods, fire and pandemic; and living for decades in a place where the natural world speaks so clearly to anyone who would listen. 'We must love one another or die', says Auden (in one version of his 'September 1, 1939'); and humans—I think, I hope—increasingly recognise that 'one another' encompasses all the things of this beautiful, broken planet.

Notes

p 13   'When the news fails' is redacted from CFA-VIC, RFS-NSW, ESA-ACT, November 2019 to February 2020.

p 71   The title is taken from Sigmund Freud's influential book of the same title (some translations render it *Studies in Hysteria*), first published in 1895 and co-authored by the physician Josef Breuer. It's often considered the work that initiated psychoanalysis, though its reception was initially, and remains, rather mixed.

p 81   *Beyond the Pleasure Principle* (1920) is Freud's exploration of factors other than pleasure-seeking that drive human behaviour; one of his more important essays, it allows consideration of the compulsion to repeat that Freud sees as a feature of neurosis.

Acknowledgements

Grateful thanks to Dr Paul Munden for his careful reading of the manuscript, and correction of an embarrassing number of typographical and literal errors. Thanks also to the members of the Prose Poetry Project, who have provided me feedback on many of the poems in this volume. Some of the poems have been published in anthologies or journals, as below.

'A history of speech', *Verity La,* November 2020

'Alternative medicine'; earlier version published as 'Tree change', *Burrow* 3, 2021

'At the Clockmakers Museum', *Not Very Quiet* 6, September 2017

'Between the media and the moment', *Meanjin* 79.2, 2020

'Beyond the Pleasure Principle', previously untitled in S Strange (ed), *Seam: Prose Poems,* Recent Work Press, 2015

'First responders', previously untitled in M Carroll & P Munden (eds), *Tract: Prose Poems,* Recent Work Press, 2017

'History for beginners', *Australian Poetry Anthology* 9, 2021–2022

'Metamorphoses' *Poetry New Zealand*, Yearbook 2, 2015

'Nature morte', *Australian Poetry Anthology* vol 8, 2020

'Refuse/refuge' and 'From the family album', in S Vasefi, Y Holt & M Smith (eds), *Borderless: A Transnational Anthology of Feminist Poetry,* 2021

'Refusing disaster (a survival plan)', *Not Very Quiet* 6, March 2020

'The passage of time', in S Strange, P Munden & A Pang (eds), *No News*, Recent Work Press, 2020

'The science of kindness', in J Kaylock & D O'Hagan (eds), *Messages from the Embers: From Devastation to Hope: Australian Bushfire Poetry Anthology*, Black Quill Press, 2020

www.ingramcontent.com/pod-product-compliance
Ingram Content Group Australia Pty Ltd
76 Discovery Rd, Dandenong South VIC 3175, AU
AUHW020639050325
407891AU00002B/8

9 780645 651324